Artist's Studio

Acting

by Jenny Fretland VanVoorst

Bullfrog Books

Ideas for Parents and Teachers

Bullfrog Books let children practice reading informational text at the earliest reading levels. Repetition, familiar words, and photo labels support early readers.

Before Reading

- Discuss the cover photo. What does it tell them?
- Look at the picture glossary together. Read and discuss the words.

Read the Book

- "Walk" through the book and look at the photos. Let the child ask questions. Point out the photo labels.
- Read the book to the child, or have him or her read independently.

After Reading

- Prompt the child to think more. Ask: Have you ever been in a play? Did you enjoy pretending to be someone else?

Bullfrog Books are published by Jump!
5357 Penn Avenue South
Minneapolis, MN 55419
www.jumplibrary.com

Library of Congress Cataloging-in-Publication Data

Names: Fretland VanVoorst, Jenny, 1972–
Title: Acting / by Jenny Fretland VanVoorst.
Description: Minneapolis, MN : Jump!, 2016. |
Series: Artist's studio |
   Includes index.
Identifiers: LCCN 2015039072 |
   ISBN 9781620312803 (hardcover: alk. paper) |
   ISBN 9781624963407 (ebook)
Subjects: LCSH: Acting—Juvenile literature.
Classification: LCC PN2086.F74 2015 |
DDC 792.02/26—dc23
LC record available at http://lccn.loc.gov/2015039072

Series Designer: Ellen Huber
Book Designer: Michelle Sonnek
Photo Researcher: Michelle Sonnek

Photo Credits: All photos by Shutterstock except: Alamy, 8; Getty Images, 13, 20–21; Igor Bulgarin/Shutterstock.com, 5, 9, 10–11; SuperStock, 14–15, 16–17; Thinkstock, 22tl.

Printed in the United States of America at Corporate Graphics in North Mankato, Minnesota.

Table of Contents

Actor's Studio 4

On the Stage 22

Picture Glossary 23

Index 24

To Learn More 24

Actor's Studio

Liz is an actor.

She is in a play.

What is her role?

She plays a queen.

Liz studies her part.
She learns her lines.

lines

She tries on
her costume.

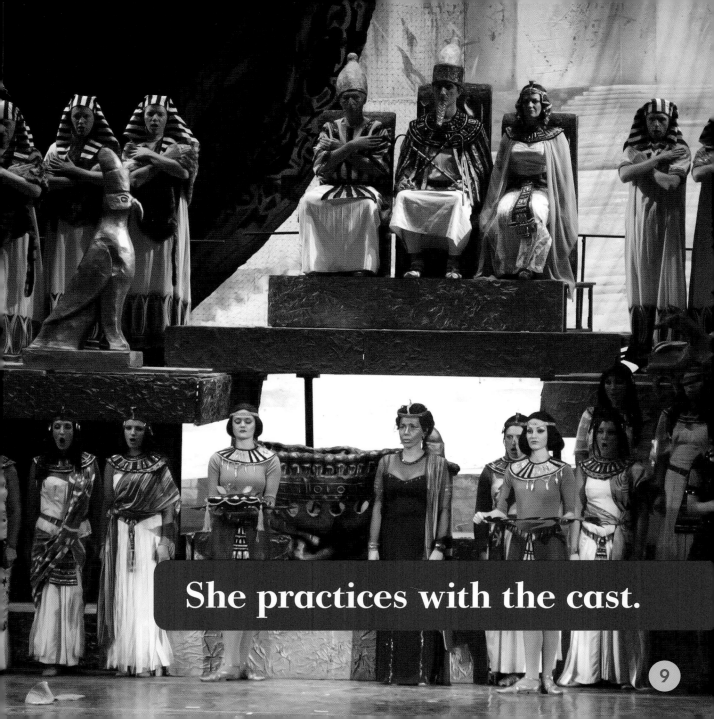

She practices with the cast.

It is time to perform.
Look! That's Liz on stage!

Ed is an actor, too.

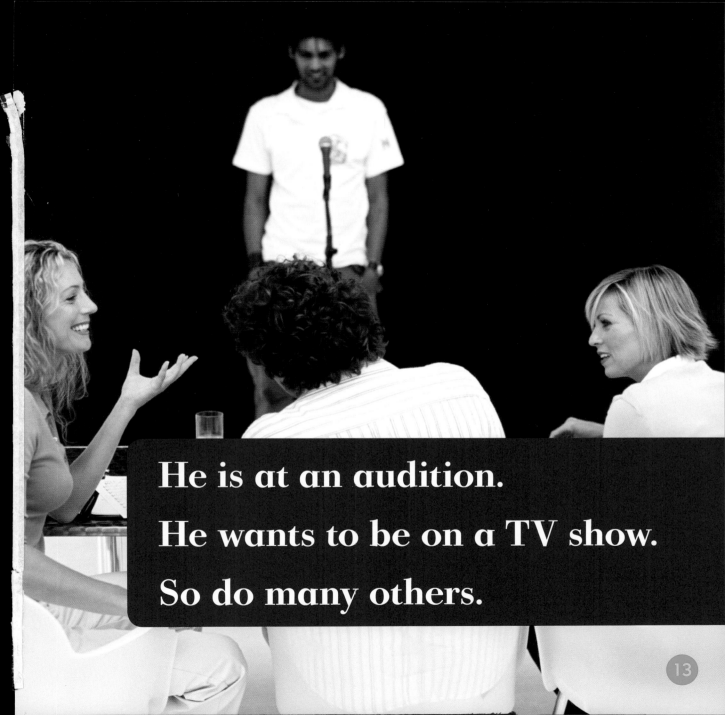

He is at an audition.

He wants to be on a TV show.

So do many others.

Ed performs a scene.

The director
gives him tips.

director

Ed tries again.

He follows the tips.

Yay! Ed got the part.
Look! That's him on TV.

Try it yourself!
Acting is fun.

On the Stage

actors

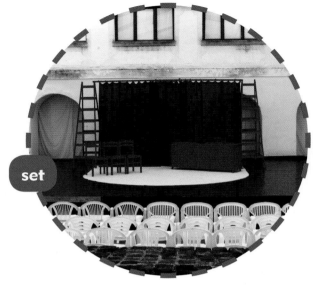

set

costumes

props

Picture Glossary

audition
A short performance to test the talents of a musician, singer, dancer, or actor.

director
The person who guides the making of a theatrical performance.

cast
The characters or the actors in a story or play.

perform
To give a show in public.

costume
Special clothing worn by actors to make them look like other people.

role
The part that a person acts in a play.

23

Index

audition 13

cast 9

costume 8

director 14

lines 6

part 6, 18

perform 11, 14

play 5

role 5

scene 14

stage 11

TV 13, 18

To Learn More

Learning more is as easy as 1, 2, 3.

1) Go to www.factsurfer.com

2) Enter "acting" into the search box.

3) Click the "Surf" button to see a list of websites.

With factsurfer.com, finding more information is just a click away.